ABCs of Acrostic Poetry

The keyword is king.

Linda Ann Nickerson

Gait
House
Press

Published in the United States by Gait House Press.

Printed in the United States of America.

2021

Cover and internal illustration/s: Public domain image.

ISBN: 978-1-7371383-1-0

ABCs of Acrostic Poetry

The keyword is king.

Linda Ann Nickerson

Dedication

ABCs of Acrostic Poetry: The keyword is king is
dedicated to every Language Arts or Creative
Writing teacher who ever put red pen
to any of my papers,
from preschool through graduate school.

You know who you are.

You challenged me and inspired me
to learn the rules well,
so I could break them effectively
when it's necessary.

And I thank you.

.

Table of Contents

Linda Ann Nickerson

Introduction

Acrostic poetry can be artistic, absorbing, and even astounding. It may also be as basic as a tower of wooden ABC blocks. It's all about the construction.

Why study acrostic poetry?

As a long-time poet, I am often asked about various poetry forms. The acrostic poem is particularly popular among those embarking on poetry writing for the first time – or those who are returning to venture into verse. Professionally, I have enjoyed teaching this poetic form.

There's something special about a simple acrostic poem.

Why do I write acrostic poetry?

Over the years, I've published blank verse, free verse (Yes, they are different.), ballads, haikus, limericks, naisaikus, sestinas, sonnets, villanelles, and other forms of poetry. Structured poetry presents a challenge that I enjoy. For example, I love a good iambic pentameter.

Acrostics offer an allure that also draws me. It's rooted in the fact that the poet must fully distill his or her topic, theme, and tone before fitting the pieces together in such a small frame.

That's a great goal and a helpful exercise for a writer, whether novice or professional.

Who will benefit from this book?

Creative writing teachers and students will find that *ABCs of Acrostic Poetry: The keyword is king* fits nicely into the acrostics unit in a poetry curriculum.

The content is arranged in workbook-style, with explanations and instructions followed by opportunities for participants to practice their own acrostic poetry craft along the way.

Writing club and creative writing workshop leaders will also discover that this resource offers an appropriate launching pad for new and practicing poets to polish their skills with acrostics.

Amazing acrostics

Poetry can be complicated or simple, ornate or basic, free-flowing or structured. From sonnets to sestinas, epics to elegies, and fancy villanelles to free verse, poetic forms are plentiful.

The acrostic poem is a super place to start, as it is one of the most straightforward forms of poetry. One might say it's as easy as A-B-C. That's not entirely true, but the idea has merit.

Acrostic poetry is poetry at its most basic. At least, that's where it begins. Consider this example:

Poem

Projecting

Original

Excerpts

Myself

Essentially, that's what poetry does. Here's another one to draw you in.

Poetry Is

Putting

Out

Earned

Thoughts

Restating

Yourself

Is

Neat.

That's pretty much why poets pen poems. It's about expression. Maybe we have stories to tell, ideas to share, pictures to paint (in words), or emotions to express.

Often, poetry brings out all of those things.

We may start with our personal journals and then see where our words take us.

Why write acrostic poetry?

Acrostic poetry is fun to write, although it can also take plenty of creativity. This poetic form makes poetry accessible to non-poets. Anyone can try his or her hand at creating an acrostic poem.

However, the most adept acrostic poets employ theme and language skillfully to design word pictures and to communicate ideas clearly and colorfully.

Acrostic poetry offers a lovely launching point for aspiring poets. (Yes, you probably tried a few of these as a kid in school.)

Trying acrostic poetry

Poets may experiment with a countless variety of acrostic forms. Popular favorites include:

- basic acrostic poetry
- end-of-line acrostics
- jumbled acrostics
- shaped acrostics

- alphabet acrostic poetry
- rhymed acrostic poetry

Let's explore each of these forms.

In the following pages (and the earlier ones), you will find several samples representing this wide variety of acrostic poetry forms.

These original poems (penned by the author of this book) are tucked in here to illustrate how different kinds of acrostics may be constructed.

For the purpose of instruction, the examples chosen for inclusion here are somewhat didactic in nature, specifically aimed at teaching the art of acrostic poetry. Some verses are unadorned and rudimentary, while others may include deeper messages or even double meanings.

Throughout this book, you will also find spaces offered (with acrostic poem prompts in place and 25 additional prompts at the end), so that you can try your own hand at writing many of the miscellaneous forms of acrostic poetry.

The full gamut is game, when it comes to writing acrostic verse. Perhaps that's why acrostic poetry finds its way into elementary school curriculum, as well as college- and graduate-level creative writing classes. The poet can make acrostic poetry as introductory or intricate as he or she desires.

Picking a topic

The secret is to select an important word (or phrase). It might be a holiday, a buzzword, or even a person's name. That becomes highlighted as the title and the theme of the acrostic poem.

This emphasized word may or may not actually appear within the body of the poem, but it can always be read vertically.

Acrostic poems have been crafted in celebration, penned in protest, scratched down in sarcasm, and tackled in tribute. Others have poked fun at popular expressions, wrestled with important life questions, or drawn attention to descriptive details of daily life.

At first pass, the fledgling writer might opt to write an acrostic poem about a treasured memory, a loved one, a personal pet, a special place, a favorite food, a sport, or a hobby.

Acrostic poets have brainstormed and gathered inspiration from fine art, favorite songs, familiar quotations, funny cartoons, and all sorts of other spots. When it comes to writing acrostic poetry, the alphabet awaits.

Highlights

How can you find

Ideas to share,

Grasping truth

Here in a poem?

Look at your life.

Identify what draws you.

Go for anything

Holding your own interest.

Tell your story.

Someone will be struck by it.

Still stuck on selecting a subject?

Creative writing workshops and classes often provide students with writing prompts. Bookstores bulge with how-tos offering numerous writing starts.

A simple internet search for blog prompts can yield helpful results as well. (Examples include Simply Snickers and The Meme Express.)

One of the benefits of using online prompts as springboards for crafting your own poems is that you can return to those websites and post links to the related poems you have created (if you publish them online).

Blog prompt participants often read and comment on one another's work this way. If you post poetry on your own blog, this can boost readership.

Once the poet has chosen the topic, it's time to build the lines around it. Now the fun begins!

Your turn:

J_____

U_____

M_____

P_____

I_____

N_____

Basic acrostic poetry

This is the simplest form of acrostic poetry and a great starting point for beginning poets and students to try.

First, pick a word (or a phrase), and write the letters in a vertical column, one letter per line. Leave an empty line space between words, if you choose to use a phrase.

Then build the poem thematically from there.

This exercise can begin in a spiral notebook or blank journal, or it can be initiated directly on a tablet or computer screen.

Let's have a little fun with the basic acrostic poetry concept. Here's a very quick example:

Fun

Find your key words,

Underline them, or put them in bold.

Now add your lines.

Notice that acrostic poems are not centered on the page. Rather, they are printed with all of their lines flush to the left, so the key word (or words) may be readily read.

Here's a slightly longer acrostic poem in this basic format.

Poetry

Perhaps you have a wonderful idea to share,

Or you may dream in colors mankind has
  never seen.

Everyone else has no idea

That you live in vibrancy unknown.

Revealing your vision can shake the world;

You simply must put it into words.

The title of an acrostic poetry is usually the word that may be read vertically, comprised of the letters with which the lines begin. In a multi-stanza acrostic, the resulting words will form a phrase. Each stanza is separated by a line-space, so the multiple words may be clearly seen.

This multi-stanza acrostic illustrates this concept.

Try It

Test your hand;

Reach for a pen.

You can write an acrostic poem.

I'll read your lines

To grasp the meaning.

Careful poets will attempt to make each initial word (the words forming the acrostic title and theme) add substance and meaning to the poem. This means trying to avoid simple filler words (such as "a," "an," "the," "for," and such) for line openings. These little words are important parts of correct language, but they add little in terms of expression or interpretation within the poem.

It's not always possible to accomplish this altogether in every acrostic poem (as seen in the poem shown above), but it's definitely a good goal.

Your turn:

B_____

R_____

A_____

V_____

E_____

Basic acrostic poetry may take at least three different forms. These poems may contain one-word lines, phrase lines, or sentence lines.

Basic acrostics: One-word lines

These are short and sweet and simple to boot. Such a poem may or may not form a complete sentence, but it ought to include a complete thought.

Word

Working

Out

Reveries

Delights.

Your turn:

P_____

L_____

A_____

Y_____

Basic acrostics: Phrase lines

Slightly more complex, these acrostics offer space for the poet to weave in imagery, wordplay, description, amplification, or even alliteration.

Ideas Count

Images beckon

Day after day

Evoking expression,

Always asking.

Someone's summoning.

Come and see.

Only observers

Understand anything,

Never to need

Tomorrow's telling.

In the example above, you may have detected that a couple of individual lines within the body of the poem are actually full sentences, even though this poem employs the phrase-lines model.

This demonstrates poetic license. Some poetry does not fit tightly within a given format.

Here's another phrase-line acrostic:

Reboot

Running wrong,

Empty of expression,

Bum start –

On and-off,

On-and-off –

There it is.

Often, phrase-line acrostic poems form complete sentences. When this occurs, these will end with periods (or question marks or exclamation marks). Then again, this is not always so.

The above example includes two matching lines, employed on purpose to deliver the central tone of the poem.

Your turn:

G_____

O_____

A_____

L_____

Basic acrostics: Full-sentence lines

Full-sentence lines are the hallmark of this acrostic form.

In some cases, a line in an acrostic poem of this form may be an independent clause, ending with a semicolon (rather than a period), joining it to the following line (which must be a related independent clause).

In terms of meaning, this is very close to using a period to end the first clause and starting the second clause as a fresh sentence. The choice is the poet's.

       Sometimes full-sentenced acrostics' titles also form complete sentences, but this is not a requirement.

Sing

Start the song.

I can hear it.

Now we join our voices.

Glad we made a joyful noise together.

       Basic acrostic poetry lines need not match for rhythm or length, as you can see in this full-sentenced example. The lines are all different lengths.

       One-and two-word lines may even be found, if they form complete sentences. Bear in mind that a sentence must include a subject and a verb. In a command (or imperative sentence), the subject may an implied "you." The acrostic poem title above ("Sing") shows this concept.

Your turn:

W_____

R_____

A_____

P_____

I_____

T_____

U_____

P_____

Again, poetic license allows the writer to mix
and match the one-word, phrase, and full-sentence

acrostic forms freely (unless a specific creative writing assignment dictates strict adherence to one form).

Here's an example of such a combination:

Mix

Mayhem

Includes merriment.

eXceptions apply.

In this little poem, the final line is not capitalized, although it begins a sentence. This has been done deliberately, so the acrostic keyword letter ("X") remains clearly identifiable by the reader..

End-of-line acrostics

This is a variation of the basic acrostic. In this format, each key word letter appears at the end of a line.

End-of-line acrostics may be written in the one-word, phrase, or full-sentence line varieties. Or they may be a blend of any or all of these forms. And they need not contain rhyme or meter. In fact, they seldom do, as that is a more difficult construction to achieve.

Poet

At the writing shoP,

You can look intO

Every poet's own eyE

And read his thoughT.

Frequently, end-of-line acrostics are formatted flush-right (or line-justified), so the key word letters line up in a vertical column on the right-hand side of the page.

The last letter of each line is capitalized and highlighted, marking the title/topic acrostic word.

In an end-of-line acrostic poem, the first letter of each line may be anything the writer selects.

Here's another end-of-line acrostic:

Linda Ann Nickerson

End

Looking asidE

Surprises wheN

Answers are found.

Your turn:

_____**T**

_____**H**

_____**O**

_____**U**

_____**G**

_____**H**

_____**T**

_____**S**

Jumbled acrostics

In some acrostic poems, the key letters may be deliberately arranged for poetic and artistic effect. This fun and frantic form of acrostic may be somewhat jarring to the reader, but it's intentionally done to fit the poet's tone, topic, mood, and meaning.

Here's what this jumbled acrostic approach might look like.

Rain, Rain

Have you eve**R** seen raind**R**ops,

Gently f**A**lling, ever f**A**lling,

Dr**I**pping all over the wet s**I**dewalk,

Whe**N** you are briskly walki**N**g off to school?

If you read downwards, you will notice the acrostic message, "Rain, Rain." In this acrostic poem, the letters are staggered, just like raindrops, as they fall. This placement is intentional. In other jumbled acrostic poems, the emphasized letters may be placed more randomly throughout each line.

Your turn:

_____**R**_____

_____**A**_____

_____**N**_____

_____**D**_____

_____**O**_____

_____**M**_____

For your turn, the RANDOM letters are arranged randomly, of course. Feel free to place them wherever they fit in your own jumbled acrostic poem. Again, these letters are capitalized and highlighted, enabling the reader to identify the title/topic key word.

Shaped acrostics

A poet may also go visual when formatting an acrostic poem, placing lines on the page to form a word picture.

Consider these examples:

- A Christmas poem might be shaped like an evergreen tree.
- A winter poem may look like a snowman.
- A Valentine poem could be molded as a heart.
- A St. Patrick's day poem might resemble a shamrock.
- An Easter poem may form a cross.
- A birthday poem might be shaped like the celebrant's initial.
- And so on.

In such a case, the acrostic poem lines might be centered on the page, aligned flush-right, or even justified. The poet selects the appropriate placement that best displays the intended shape of the poem.

Here's a very simple pyramid acrostic poem.

Look Up

Lo!

Onlookers,

Only observe.

Kicking conventions and

Understanding unfathomabilities

Perhaps produces more poignant perspectives.

Your turn:

C_____

A_____

N_____

Y_____

O_____

U_____

S_____

E_____

E_____

I_____

T_____

As you create your own shaped acrostic, you will determine the line lengths needed to form the image you desire, visually representing the theme of your poem.

Alphabet acrostic poetry

This form of verse is a little trickier. Each alphabet acrostic poem contains 26 lines, and each line begins with a different letter of the alphabet (in sequence).

Here's an alphabet acrostic poem about writing acrostic poetry.

A to Z

Acrostic poetry is fun to write,

Because nearly anyone

Can do it.

Describing acrostic poetry is simple:

Everyone knows the alphabet.

Finding ways to start each line is tricky.

Good writers will reach for great words.

How many lines will the poem have?

In most cases, alphabet acrostics have 26,

Just one line for each letter.

Keeping the words straight,

Lined up in neat columns,

Makes all the difference.

Now others can read the alphabet

Only by looking at the first letters.

Poetry is fun, if you know how.

Quite a few people enjoy

Reading and writing creative verse.

Simply putting pen to paper

Takes ideas and insight.

Understanding poetry

Very often is trickier.

When we take time to ponder it,

e**X**amining imagery, poetry may

Yield something of beauty,

Zooming in on truth.

For the record, let's just agree that it's OK to sneak the "X" into an "eX-word. Poetry is a creative endeavor, and sometimes the rules can be intentionally blurred for the sake of the artistic composition.

Alphabet acrostic poems may be constructed with word, phrase, or full-sentence lines. Any combination of these is also acceptable. These poems may include rhyme or meter, but they most frequently do not.

Your turn:

A_____

B_____

C_____

D_____

E_____

F_____

G_____

H_____

I_____

J_____

K_____

L_____

M_____

N_____

O_____

P_____

Q_____

R_____

S_____

T_____

U_____

V_____

W_____

X_____

Y_____

Z_____

Rhymed acrostic poetry

This type of acrostic poetry is considerably more complex. Poets seeking an extra challenge may find this even more appealing.

Essentially, rhymed acrostic poetry follows the basic structural format for acrostic poetry, but the lines are both metered and rhymed. As with all well-crafted rhymed poetry, the rhyming words should be significant, usually adding substance to the poem.

Writers receive extra points, figuratively speaking, for multi-syllabic rhymes. Examples include "poem" and "know 'em" in the following "Rhyme" poem, plus "hurry" and "flurry" in the "Read" one.

Poets may exercise creative license with

occasional words for improved flow, readability, dialect, emphasis, rhythm, or rhyme.

Take a look at the following verse, in which "them" becomes "'em." In an acrostic poem titled "Aloud" (see page 38), the word "offering" was changed to "off'ring" to drop a syllable for rhythmic fit.

It's also possible for the poet to craft imaginary or intentionally altered words for the sake of clever rhyming. For example, to rhyme with "dunk" or "funk" at the end of a line, a poet might change "think" to "thunk."

This is a rhymed acrostic limerick poem, using the standard five-line limerick format. (Notice the AABBA rhyme scheme and the limerick meter.)

Rhyme

Regarding an A-B-C poem,

Have echoes in mind, if you know 'em.

Your lines, they may flow.

Most readers will know

Each stanza contains its own gem.

Rhymed acrostics may feature various metric formats and rhyme schemes. The following example has an AABB rhyme scheme.

Ring

Rhythm and rhyme,

Intoned in true time,

Nicely abide,

Good readers to guide.

The next rhymed acrostic features an ABAB rhyme scheme.

Read

Reach for a book;

Everyone, hurry.

After a look,

Dreams fly a-flurry.

Rhyme schemes can also be more complex , as

in this acrostic example, which is ABCABCA:

Complex

Coupled in pairs for to rhyme,

Offset by a turn of a phrase,

Most poetry be tightly fit,

Portending import in its prime.

Look closely across and lengthways;

Each poem acrostic will fit,

eXcept when the poet adds time.

Your turn:

L_____

E_____

T_____

S_____

G_____

O_____

A few technicalities

Page layouts are key, when posting or publishing acrostic poetry. It's important to keep a full stanza contained on a single page, if possible (or at least, on a single page spread). Otherwise, readers may struggle to read the column and catch the acrostic.

This is not the case for alphabet acrostic poetry, which (by definition) contains 26 lines and can be difficult to fit on a single page.

Often, the acrostic letters in a poem are enlarged, bolded, or otherwise highlighted for added emphasis. Plenty of acrostic poets employ this during the writing process, removing the accentuation before publication. Others leave it in place to draw visual attention to these initial characters. (In this book, these key letters remain enlarged for added teachability.)

Whether these key letters appear at the line beginnings (usually), line endings, or elsewhere, they are capitalized.

As a side note, punctuation is often optional within acrostic poetry. It may be omitted in many cases, unless it is needed for clarity. The mid-poem use of periods and commas is up to the poet. Acrostic poems with longer lines may warrant punctuation. A question mark may be difficult to avoid, if the poem raises a query.

However, if the acrostic poem forms a full sentence, it's appropriate to put a period at the end.

The importance of punctuation may be debated, particularly by editors and writing instructors. This is another instance in which creative writers periodically bend the rules strategically for aesthetic effect.

Pointers for public readings

Poetry is best read aloud, whether in company or solitude. This allows readers/listeners to grasp the pace, rhythm, and flow of each line. This is especially important with rhymed/metered poems.

When silence is required (as when reading in a library, study hall, or other quiet space), poetry readers often speak out the words to themselves, without using actual voice.

Aloud

Anyone interested?

Lend an ear,

Off'ring to hear

Untold words,

Delivered and clear.

For acrostic poetry readings (such as poetry readings, writing groups, open mic nights, audiobooks, videos, or podcasts), it may be wise to provide printed or electronic copies for audiences. This allows listeners to identify easily the line beginnings (or endings) that form the acrostic key word or phrases and to appreciate each poem's visual nature.

Your turn:

L_____

I_____

S_____

T_____

E_____

N_____

Once you've written yours, try reading it aloud.

Conclusion

Like every poetic form, acrostic poetry allows writers to express themselves with allegory, alliteration, allusion, imagery, irony, metaphor, motif, parody, personification, or other literary devices. Poems may be comical, confessional, devotional, dramatic, fictional, figurative, functional, futuristic, literal, romantic, symbolic, or whatever the poet chooses. Be original!

Feisty Original

Finding fresh phrases to fall

Ends every so often in excess.

Imagined ironies also increase insights,

Sometimes strengthening resolve.

Try these turns of phrases;

Yielded imports may bring a bounty.

Outlandish or odd, fact or fancy,

Rhymed or random, language brings learning.

Insights and delights vie for attention,

Gaining ground and ceding space.

Ideas are creative chatter or dull debris.

No one knows until verses are voiced.

Audible readings add power to poetry.

Listen, and you may live a little.

All in all, acrostic poetry is a super place to start.

25 Poetry Practice Prompts

Here's your chance to practice your newfound or rediscovered skill at creating acrostic poetry. Pick a prompt, and see where it takes you. Remember: You can place your acrostic key word vertically at the beginning or end of your poetry lines, or scatter the letters randomly to form an artistic pattern.

Believer

_____

_____

_____

_____

_____

_____

_____

Bounce

_____

_____

_____

_____

_____

_____

Careful

_____

_____

_____

_____

_____

_____

Dinosaur

_____

_____

_____

_____

_____

_____

_____

Friends

_____

_____

_____

_____

_____

_____

_____

Go Ahead

Golden

Hearing

_____

_____

_____

_____

_____

_____

History

_____

_____

_____

_____

_____

Horrors

Jester

Kid

_____

_____

_____

Low

_____

_____

_____

Maybe

_____

_____

_____

_____

_____

Messenger

_____

_____

_____

_____

_____

_____

_____

_____

_____

Oxygen

_____

_____

_____

_____

_____

_____

Pretends

_____

_____

_____

_____

_____

_____

_____

Prime Time

_____

_____

_____

_____

_____

_____

_____

_____

_____

Risk

_____

_____

_____

_____

Rugged

_____

_____

_____

_____

_____

_____

Starts

_____

_____

_____

_____

_____

Time Out

_____

_____

_____

_____

_____

_____

_____

Linda Ann Nickerson

Why Not

_____

_____

_____

_____

_____

_____

Wishful

_____

_____

_____

_____

_____

_____

Windup

_____

_____

_____

_____

_____

_____

Poems Included

(in order of appearance)

A to Z

Rhyme

Ring

Read

Complex

Aloud

Feisty Original

All acrostic poems contained in this book are
original and copyrighted by the author. (All rights
reserved.)

Linda Ann Nickerson

About the Author

An award-winning poet and prolific writer, holding a B.A. in English and an M.S. in Journalism, Linda Ann Nickerson has worked as a professional writer for more than four decades.

She has also taught creative writing, poetry, and literature classes and has presented to adult writing workshops and groups.

In an earlier life, she worked as a book editor and widely-read reviewer of books on all types of topics.

Linda Ann writes news and feature columns for several well-known websites. Her published portfolio includes well over 5,000 web articles, as well as countless print pieces.

When she's not writing poetry, fiction, news, features, or promotional copy, Linda Ann may be found riding horses, running canine cross-country, biking country trails, stitching up a quilt, or training for her next marathon. Or she may simply have her nose buried in another book.

Other poetry books by Linda Ann Nickerson include:

- *Absent Nightmare Zinnias: Rhymed Acrostics from A to Z*

- *Fashion Victims: Missing Style by a Marvelous Mile*

- *Going Vertical: Acrostics in Action*

- *Horseplay Secrets: Learning in Rhyme from Equines Sublime*

- *Stealing Wonder: A Rhyming Race to Capture Grace*

- *What's in Santa's Sleigh This Christmas?*